SCIENTOLOGY
Making the World a Better Place

M000168837

Founded and developed by L. Ron Hubbard, Scientology is an applied religious philosophy which offers an exact route through which anyone can regain the truth and simplicity of his spiritual self.

Scientology consists of specific axioms that define the underlying causes and principles of existence and a vast area of observations in the humanities, a philosophic body that literally applies to the entirety of life.

This broad body of knowledge resulted in two applications of the subject: first, a technology for man to increase his spiritual awareness and attain the freedom sought by many great philosophic teachings; and, second, a great number of fundamental principles men can use to improve their lives. In fact, in this second application, Scientology offers nothing less than practical methods to better *every* aspect of our existence—means to create new ways of life. And from this comes the subject matter you are about to read.

Compiled from the writings of L. Ron Hubbard, the data presented here is but one of the tools which can be found in *The Scientology Handbook*. A comprehensive guide, the handbook contains numerous applications of Scientology which can be used to improve many other areas of life.

In this booklet, the editors have augmented the data with a short introduction, practical exercises and examples of successful application.

Courses to increase your understanding and further materials to broaden your knowledge are available at your nearest Scientology church or mission, listed at the back of this booklet.

Many new phenomena about man and life are described in Scientology, and so you may encounter terms in these pages you are not familiar with. These are described the first time they appear and in the glossary at the back of the booklet.

Scientology is for use. It is a practical philosophy, something one *does*. Using this data, you *can* change conditions.

Millions of people who want to do something about the conditions they see around them have applied this knowledge. They know that life can be improved. And they know that Scientology works.

Use what you read in these pages to help yourself and others and you will too.

CHURCH OF SCIENTOLOGY INTERNATIONAL

How does one get things done? How does one make a dream a reality or carry a plan through to completion? Many of us seem to have unrealized goals or incomplete plans and many of us face tasks that appear overwhelming, even impossible to achieve. This is true not only of individuals, but of companies and even countries. History is filled with failed projects.

In examining the subject of organization, L. Ron Hubbard developed an enormous body of technology to ensure the success of any group. In doing so, he also provided a solution to the most common of failings: the lack of ability to execute plans.

*In this booklet, you will discover how to attain literally any goal, large or small. Plans **can** be carried through to fruition, but a number of vital steps must be taken, one after the other. You'll learn what these steps are and how to apply them to anything—a personal ambition, a family, a group, a business and more. You'll learn that your dreams can become real.* ■

ADMINISTRATIVE SCALE

T he achievement of one's goals, no matter how large or small the endeavor, relies on goals, purposes and activities being aligned and organized.

A goal is not something that one decides upon which then miraculously comes to fruition, just because one decided it would. The attainment of a goal necessitates that certain actions be carried out in the real world which effect some change for the better and a step closer toward its accomplishment.

One can be working toward a goal, but discover that his actions do not yield any forward progress. This occurs not only for an individual in his life, but also for an organization, state or country of any size. This can be a result of the plans, actions and other factors not being aligned to attain the goal.

There are actually a number of subjects that make up an activity. Each of these must operate in a coordinated manner to achieve success in the intended accomplishment of the envisioned goal.

A scale has been developed in Scientology which gives a sequence (and relative seniority) of subjects relating to organization.

GOALS	A *goal* is a known objective toward which actions are directed with the purpose of achieving that end.
PURPOSES	A *purpose* is a lesser goal applying to specific activities or subjects. It often expresses future intentions.
POLICY	*Policy* consists of the operational rules or guides for the organization which are not subject to change.
PLANS	A *plan* is a short-range broad intention thought up for the handling of a broad area to remedy it or expand it, or to obstruct or impede an opposition to expansion.
PROGRAMS	A *program* is a series of steps in sequence to carry out a plan.
PROJECTS	A *project* is a sequence of steps written to carry out *one* step of a program.
ORDERS	An *order* is a verbal or written direction to carry out a program step or apply general policy.
IDEAL SCENES	An *ideal scene* expresses what a scene or area ought to be. If one has not envisioned an ideal scene with which to compare the existing scene, he will not be able to recognize departures from it.
STATISTICS	A *statistic* is a number or amount compared to an earlier number or amount of the same thing. Statistics refer to the quantity of work done or the value of it.
VALUABLE FINAL PRODUCTS	A *valuable final product* is a product that can be exchanged for the services or goods of the society.

This scale is worked up and worked down UNTIL IT IS (EACH ITEM) IN FULL AGREEMENT WITH THE REMAINING ITEMS.

In short, for success, all these items in the scale must agree with all other items in the scale on the same subject.

Let us take "golf balls" as a subject for the scale. Then all these scale items must be in agreement with one another on the subject of golf balls. It is an interesting exercise.

The scale also applies in a destructive subject. Like "cockroaches."

When an item in the scale is *not* aligned with the other items, the project will be hindered, if not fail.

The skill with which all these items in any activity are aligned and gotten into action is called MANAGEMENT.

Group members only become upset when one or more of these points are not aligned to the rest and at least some group agreement.

Groups appear slow, inefficient, unhappy, inactive or quarrelsome only when these items are not aligned, made known and coordinated.

Any activity can be improved by debugging or aligning this scale in relation to the group activity.

As lack of agreement breeds lessened communication and lessened affinity, it follows that unreal items on the scale (not aligned) produce upsets and disaffection.

It then follows that when these scale items are well aligned with each other and the group, there will be high agreement, high communication and high affinity in the group.

Group mores aligned so and followed by the group gives one an ethical group and also establishes what will then be considered as harmful, contrasurvival acts in the group by group members.

This scale and its parts and ability to line them up are one of the most valuable tools of organization.

Making Planning an Actuality

For an individual, group or organization to achieve an intended goal requires knowledge of certain principles on the subject of organization.

When we look at organization in its most simple form, when we seek certain key actions or circumstances that make organization work, when we need a very simple, very vital rundown to teach people that will produce results, we find only a few points we need to stress.

The purpose of organization is TO MAKE PLANNING BECOME ACTUALITY.

An actuality is a state or thing that exists in reality.

Organization is not just a fancy, complex system, done for its own sake. That is bureaucracy at its worst. Graphs for the sake of graphs, rules for the sake of rules, only add up to failures.

The only virtue (not always a bad one) of a complex, unwieldy, meaningless bureaucratic structure is that it provides jobs for the friends of those in control. If it does not also bring about burdensome taxation and threatened bankruptcy by reason of the expense of maintaining it, and if it does not saddle a people or production employees with militant (aggressive) inspections and needless control, organization for the sake of providing employment is not evil but beyond providing employment is useless, and only when given too much authority is it destructive.

The kings of France and other lands used to invent titles and duties to give activity to the hordes of noble hangers-on to keep them at court, under surveillance, and out of mischief out in the provinces where they might stir up their own people. "Keeper of the Footstools," "Holder of the Royal Nightgown" and other such titles were fought for, bought, sold and held with ferocity.

Status-seeking, the effort to become more important and have a personal reason for being and for being respected, gets in the road of honest efforts to effectively organize in order to get something done, in order to make something economically sound.

Organization for its own sake, in actual practice, usually erects a monster that becomes so hard to live with that it becomes overthrown. Production losses, high taxes, irritating or fearsome interference with the people or actual producers invites and accomplishes bankruptcy or revolt, usually both, even in commercial companies.

Therefore to be meaningful, useful and lasting, an organization (corporation, company, business, group, etc.) has to fit into the definition above:

TO MAKE PLANNING BECOME ACTUALITY.

In companies and countries there is no real lack of dreaming. All but the most depraved (morally bad or corrupt) heads of companies or states wish to see specific or general improvement. This is also true of their executives and, as it forms the basis of nearly all revolts, it is certainly true of workers. From top to bottom, then, there is, in the large majority, a desire for improvement.

More food, more profit, more pay, more facilities and, in general, more and better of whatever they believe is good or beneficial. This also includes less of what they generally consider to be bad.

Programs which obtain general support consist of more of what is beneficial and less of what is detrimental. "More food, less disease," "more beautiful buildings, less hovels," "more leisure, less work," "more activity, less unemployment," are typical of valuable and acceptable programs.

But only to have a program is to have only a dream. In companies, in political parties, useful programs are very numerous. They suffer only from a lack of execution.

All sorts of variations of program failure occur. The program is too big. It is not generally considered desirable. It is not needed at all. It would benefit only a few. Such are surface reasons. The basic reason is lack of organization know-how.

Any program, too ambitious, partially acceptable, needed or not needed, could be put into effect if properly organized.

The five-year plans of some nations which were in vogue were almost all very valuable and almost all fell short of their objectives. The reason was not that they were unreal, too ambitious or generally unacceptable. The reason for any such failure was and is lack of organization.

It is not man's dreams that fail him. It is the lack of know-how required to bring those dreams into actuality.

Good administration has two distinct targets:

1. To perpetuate (prolong the existence of) an existing company, culture or society,

2. To make planning become actuality.

Given a base on which to operate—which is to say land, people, equipment and a culture—one needs a good administrative pattern of some sort just to maintain it.

Thus (1) and (2) above become (2) only. The plan is "to continue the existing entity." No company or country continues unless one continues to put it there. Thus an administrative system of some sort, no matter how crude, is necessary to perpetuate any group or any subdivision of a group. Even a king or headman or manager who has no other supporting system to whom one can bring disputes about land or water or pay is an administrative system. The foreman of a labor gang that only loads trucks has an astonishingly complex administrative system at work.

Companies and countries do not work just because they are there or because they are traditional. They are continuously put there by one or another form of administration.

When a whole system of administration moves out or gets lost or forgotten, collapse occurs unless a new or substitute system is at once moved into place.

Changing the head of a department, much less a general manager and much, much less a ruler, can destroy a portion or the whole since the old system, unknown, disregarded or forgotten, may cease and no new system which is understood is put in its place. Frequent transfers within a company or country can keep the entire group small, disordered and confused, since such transfers destroy what little administration there might have been.

Thus, if administrative shifts or errors or lack can collapse any type of group, it is vital to know the basic subject of organization.

Even if the group is at effect—which is to say originates nothing but only defends in the face of threatened disaster—it still must plan. And if it plans, somehow it must get the plan executed or done. Even a simple situation of an attacked fortress has to be defended by planning and doing the plan, no matter how crude. The order "Repel the invader who is storming the south wall" is the result of observation and planning no matter how brief or unthorough. Getting the south wall defended occurs by some system of administration even if it only consists of sergeants hearing the order and pushing their men to the south wall.

A company with heavy debts has to plan even if it is just to stall off creditors. And some administrative system has to exist even to do only that.

The terrible dismay of a young leader who plans a great and powerful new era only to find himself dealing with old and weak faults is attributable not to his "foolish ambition" or "lack of reality" but to his lack of organizational know-how.

Even elected presidents or prime ministers of democracies are victims of such terrible dismay. They do not, as is routinely asserted, "go back on their campaign promises" or "betray the people." They, as well as their members of parliament, simply lack the rudiments (fundamentals) of organizational know-how. They cannot put their campaign promises into effect, not because they are too high-flown (sounding grand or important) but because they are politicians, not administrators.

To some men it seems enough to dream a wonderful dream. Just because they dreamed it they feel it should now take place. They become very provoked when it does not occur.

Whole nations, to say nothing of commercial firms or societies or groups, have spent decades in floundering turmoil because the basic dreams and plans were never brought to fruition (successful completion).

Whether one is planning for the affluence of the Appalachian Mountains or a new loading shed closer to the highway, the gap between the plan and the actuality will be found to be lack of administrative know-how.

Technical ignorance, finance, even lack of authority and unreal planning itself are none of them true barriers between planning and actuality.

PLANS AND PROGRAMS

There is, however, much to know of the techniques employed to draw up planning which will bring one's dreams to realization. An initial step would be to comprehend the basic terms relating to the subject.

A *plan* is a description of the short-range broad intentions as to what one sees is required to handle a specific area. A plan would be expected to remedy nonoptimum circumstances in an area or expand it or to obstruct or impede an opposition to expansion.

For a plan to be carried out requires it be broken down into the specific actions necessary to accomplish what the plan intends to do. This is done by use of a *program*.

A *program* is a series of steps in sequence to carry out a plan. To write a program requires that a plan exist beforehand, even if only in the mind of the person writing the program. A step of a program is called a *target*.

A program is composed of targets. A *target* is an action which should be undertaken in order to achieve a desired objective.

There are several *values* of targets. Not all targets are the same value or importance. Each of these is described below.

Major Target

A *major target* is the desirable overall ambition being undertaken. This is highly generalized, such as "to become a trained Scientology practitioner."

Other examples in different fields would be:

"To get all machinery and equipment in the company operational."

"To acquire, set up, make ready and use a suitable property and facilities at reasonable low cost."

"To get books being distributed to mail order customers and any stores or distributors."

A major target is the overall objective.

Primary Targets

A *primary target* is one which deals with the organizational, personnel and communication-type steps that have to be kept in. These are a group of "understood" targets which, if overlooked, bring about inaction.

The first of these is: SOMEBODY THERE

Then: WORTHWHILE PURPOSE

Then: SOMEBODY TAKING RESPONSIBILITY FOR THE AREA OR ACTION

Then: FORM OF ORGANIZATION PLANNED WELL

Then: FORM OF ORGANIZATION HELD OR REESTABLISHED

Then: ORGANIZATION OPERATING

If we have the above "understood" targets, we can go on; *but if these drop out or are not substituted for,* then no matter what targets are set thereafter they will go rickety or fail entirely.

In the above there may be a continual necessity to reassert one or more of the "understood" targets WHILE trying to get further *targets* going.

Some examples of primary targets would be:

"Accept the job to which one is being assigned."

"Read and understand the program which you will be doing."

You'll do very well as my chief mechanic.

Somebody there is an example of a primary target.

Vital Targets

A *vital target* is something that must be done to operate at all.

This requires an inspection of both the area one is operating into and the factors or materiel or organization with which we are operating.

One then finds those points (sometimes *while* operating) which stop or threaten future successes. And sets the overcoming of the vital ones as targets.

Some examples of these would be:

"Look into the circumstances one is inspecting with your own eyes; don't accept another's report."

"Accept no orders from anyone other than your direct senior."

"Do not let the supply of books falter in the country while the campaign is ongoing."

"Maintain a high level of ethical behavior and set an excellent example in doing so."

A vital target must be in to operate successfully.

Always keep these lights on during working hours.

14

Conditional Targets

A *conditional target* is one which is done to find out data, or if a project can be done, where it can be done, etc.

You've seen chaps work all their lives to "get rich" or some such thing in order to "tour the world" and never make it. Some other fellow sets "tour the world" and goes directly at it and *does* it. So there is a type of target known as a *conditional* target: If I could just _____ then we could _____ and so accomplish _____. This is all right of course until it gets unreal.

There is a whole class of conditional targets that have no IF in them. These are legitimate targets. They have lots of WILL in them, "We *will* _____ and then _____."

Sometimes sudden "breaks" show up and one must quickly take advantage of them. This is only "good luck." One uses it and replans quickly when it *happens*. One is on shaky ground to count on "good luck" as a solution.

A valid conditional target would be:

"We will go there and see if the area is useful."

Another example of a conditional target is:

"If there is a backlog of filing, then organize a short time period each day where the company's employees assist in filing the particles in the correct files."

All conditional targets are basically actions of gathering data first, and if it is okay, then go into action.

If we get that busy, I'll install a second bay.

All conditional targets are basically actions of gathering data first, and if it is okay, then go into action.

Operating Targets

An *operating target* is one which would set the *direction* of advance and qualify it. It normally includes a scheduled *time* by which it has to be complete so as to fit into other targets.

Sometimes the time is set as "BEFORE." And there may be no time for the event that it must be done "before." Thus it goes into a rush basis "just in case."

Examples of operating targets would be:

"Advertise books in local magazines which are subscribed to by the type of audience who would be interested in these books."

"Hire local labor to make adobe bricks for the walls."

"Establish how the company newsletter can be most inexpensively mailed to the branch offices."

"Clean up the President's suite."

"Send a courier with the return mail direct to the home office."

*An **operating target** would set the direction of advance and qualify it.*

Production Targets

Setting quotas, usually against time, are *production* targets.

Examples of production targets would be:

"Next year's tuition set aside by June."

"Fifty thousand books bound by next month."

As *statistics* most easily reflect production, an organization or activity can be so PRODUCTION TARGET conscious that it fails to set conditional, operating or primary targets. When this happens, then production is liable to collapse for lack of planning stated in other types of targets.

Production as the only target type can become so engulfing that conditional targets even when set are utterly neglected. Then operating and primary targets get very unreal and statistics go DOWN.

YOU HAVE TO INSPECT AND SURVEY AND GATHER DATA AND SET OPERATING AND PRIMARY TARGETS BEFORE YOU CAN SET PRODUCTION TARGETS.

A normal reason for down statistics on production is the vanishment of primary targets. These go out and nobody notices that this affects production badly. Production depends on other prior targets being kept *in*.

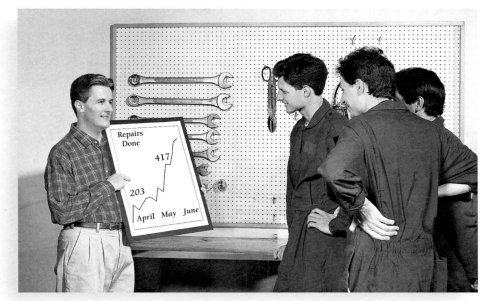

*Setting quotas, usually against time, are **production targets**.*

The following is a concise summary of the different types of targets which make up a program.

Types of Targets

MAJOR TARGETS	The broad general ambition, possibly covering a long, only approximated period of time. Such as "To attain greater security" or "To get the organization up to fifty employees."
PRIMARY TARGETS	The organizational, personnel, communication-type targets. These have to be kept *in*. These are the type of targets which deal with the terminals, communication routes, materiel and organizing boards. Example: "To put someone in charge of organizing it and have him set remaining primary targets." Or "To reestablish the original communication system which has dropped out."
VITAL TARGETS	Those which must be done to operate at all, based on an inspection of the area in which one is operating.
CONDITIONAL TARGETS	Those which set up EITHER/OR, to find out data or if a project can be done or where or to whom.
OPERATING TARGETS	Those which lay out directions and actions or a schedule of events or timetable.
PRODUCTION TARGETS	Those which set quantities like statistics.

WRITING PROGRAM TARGETS

A few data must be kept in mind when writing targets for a program. Applying these will assist one to get his programs done and bring his plans to actuality.

When writing operating targets, the first one must require the person, area or organization increase its level of production.

However, in actual fact, you can't write an operating target that is pure production. It would be impossible to write such a target because somebody would have to do it, and the moment that you have somebody there to do it, you have organization. So there is a certain amount of organization that comes into it.

For example, in handling a department responsible for collecting the organization's income, one would have to include in it, as its second target, beefing up the department. The first target would be for the department to do anything it could to handle its collections. And the second target would be to beef up that department forthwith. Otherwise, the production would not continue.

So there has to be immediate organization for production.

Terminable Targets

Now, how do you like a target like this: "Maintain friendly relations with the environment." How do you like that target? It is utterly, completely not a target that gets the person to carry out an action. It isn't a target at all!

Now, if it said, "Call on so and so, and so and so, and make them aware of your presence…" and so forth, it could have a DONE on it.

Targets should be terminable—doable, finishable, completable. This will contribute to the success of one's programs.

Sample Programs

Having learned the types of targets and how to write them, one can then formulate programs.

On the following pages you will find two sample programs. They clearly show the interrelationship and sequence of the different target types which make up a standard program. Each sample has a specific purpose: with the first, one learns how to do a project; with the second, one learns about production. One can do these two programs, target by target, and understand the orderliness and workability of programs and above all, what the types of targets are and how they work together.

By doing these programs, you will then be able to write and carry out your own programs and that will set you firmly on the road to accomplishing your goals and purposes.

Sample Program #1

Purpose: To learn to do a program.

Major Target: To get it done.

Primary Target:

1. Read this program.

Vital Targets:

1. Be honest about doing this.
2. Do all of it.
3. Check off each one when done.

Operating Targets:

1. Take off your right shoe. Look at the sole. Note what's on it. Put it back on.
2. Go get a drink of water.
3. Take a sheet of paper. Draw three concentric circles on it. Turn it over face down. Write your name on the back. Tear it up and put the scraps in a book.
4. Take off your left shoe. Look at the sole. Note what is on it. Put it back on.
5. Go find someone and say hello. Return and write a message to yourself as to how they received it.
6. Take off both shoes and bang the heels together three times and put them back on.
7. Write a list of projects in your life you have left incomplete or not done.
8. Write why this was.
9. Check this program carefully to make sure you have honestly done it all.
10. List your realizations, if any, while doing this program.
11. Decide whether you have honestly done this program.

Sample Program #2

Purpose: To learn about production.

Major Target: To actually produce something.

Primary Targets:

1. Get a pencil and five sheets of paper.

2. Situate yourself so you can do this program.

Vital Targets:

1. Read an operating target and be sure to do it all before going on.

2. Actually produce what's called for.

Operating Targets:

1. Look very busy without actually doing anything.

2. Do it again but this time be very convincing.

3. Work out the product of your job or activity. Get help from another person as needed.

4. Straighten up the papers on your desk.

5. Take sheet 1 as per primary targets above. Write whether or not No. 4 was production.

6. Find a paper or message that doesn't contribute in any way to your getting out your own product.

7. Answer it.

8. Take the second sheet called for in the primary target. Write on it why the action in 7 is perfectly reasonable.

9. Take the third sheet of paper and draw out how you receive communication on your job.

10. Get out one correct product for your job, complete, of high quality.

11. Deliver it.

12. Review the operating targets and see which one made you feel best.

13. Take the fourth sheet of paper and write down whether or not production is the basis of morale.

14. Take the fifth sheet of paper, use it for a cover sheet and write a summary of the program.

15. Realize you have completed a program.

Planning and Targets

All manner of plans can be drawn up to accomplish desirable ends. However, they are just plans. Until the when and how they will be done and by whom has been established, scheduled, authorized or agreed upon, they will not be completed.

This is why planning sometimes gets a bad name.

You could *plan* to make a million dollars but if when, how and who were not set in program form as targets of different types, it just wouldn't happen. A brilliant plan is drawn as to *how* to convert Boston Harbor into a fuel tanker area. It could be on drawings with everything perfectly placed. One could even have models of it. Ten years go by and it has not been started much less completed. You have seen such plans. World's fairs are full of them.

One could also have a plan which was targeted in program form—who, when, how—and if the targets were poor or unreal, it would never be completed.

One can also have a plan which had no CONDITIONAL TARGET ahead of it and so no one really wanted it and it served no purpose really. It is unlikely it would ever be finished. Such a thing existed in Corfu (an island off Greece). It was a half-completed Greek theater which had just been left that way. No one had asked the inhabitants if they wanted it or if it was needed. So even though very well planned and even partially targeted and half-completed, there it is—half-finished. And has remained that way.

A plan, by which is meant the drawing or scale modeling of some area, project or thing, is of course a vital necessity in any construction and construction fails without it. It can even be okayed *as a plan*.

But if it was not the result of findings of a conditional target (a survey of what's needed or feasible), it will be useless or won't fit in. And if no funds are allocated to it and no one is ordered to do it and if no scheduling of doing it exists, then on each separate count it won't ever be done.

Where one has worked out a plan and is devising a program requiring approval, to get them okayed, one would have to show it as:

a. A result of a conditional target (survey of what's wanted and needed),

b. The details of the thing itself, meaning a picture of it or its scope plus the ease or difficulty in doing it and with what persons or materials,

c. Classification of it as vital or simply useful,

d. The primary targets of it showing the organization needed to do it,

e. The operating targets showing its scheduling (even if scheduled not with dates but days or weeks) and dovetailing with other actions,

f. Its cost and whether or not it will pay for itself or can be afforded or how much money it will make.

The program would have to include the targets.

A *plan* would be the *design* of the thing itself.

Thus we see why some things don't come off at all and why they often don't get completed even when planned. The plan is not put forward in its *target* framework and so is unreal or doesn't get done.

Sometimes a conditional target fails to ask what obstacles or opposition would be encountered or what skills are available and so can go off the rails in that fashion.

But if these points are grasped, then one sees the scope of the subject and can become quite brilliant and achieve things hitherto out of reach or never thought of before.

STRATEGIC PLANNING

No study of planning and targets is complete without examining the subject of strategic planning. It is of such vital importance that it merits an in-depth study as to its definition and use as well as its relationship to other aspects of management.

The term "STRATEGY" is derived from the Greek words:

strategos, which means "general,"

stratos, which means "army,"

agein, meaning "to lead."

STRATEGY, therefore, by dictionary definition, refers to a plan for the overall conduct of a war or sector of it.

By extrapolation (inferring from known facts), it has also come to mean a plan for the skillful overall conduct of a large field of operations, or a sector of such operations, toward the achievement of a specific goal or result.

This is planning that is done at upper-echelon level, as, if it is to be effective, it must be done from an overview of the broad existing situation.

It is a statement of the intended plans for accomplishing a broad objective and inherent in its definition is the idea of clever use of resources or maneuvers for outwitting the enemy or overcoming existing obstacles to win the objective.

It is the central strategy worked out at the top which, like an umbrella, covers the activities of the echelons below it.

That tells us what strategic planning is.

What It Does

What strategic planning does is provide direction for the activities of all the lower echelons. All the tactical plans and programs and projects to be carried out at lower echelons in order to accomplish the objective stream down from the strategic plan at the top. It is the overall plan against which all of these are coordinated.

This gives a clear look at why strategic planning is so vitally important and why it must be done by the upper-level planning body if management is to be effective and succeed.

What happens if strategic planning is missing? Well, what happens in the conduct of a war if no strategic planning is done?

Key troops can be left unflanked and unsupported in key areas while other troops fight aimless battles at some minor outpost. Supplies and ammunition could be deployed (positioned for use) to the wrong area or not forwarded at all. Conflict of orders, jammed lines and maneuvers, wasted resources and lost battles all result. With the lack of a plan, coordination is missing and it's a scene of confusion and dispersal. In short, disaster.

What a difference between this and a strong, coordinated, positive thrust toward attaining the objective!

Transposing all of this over into our own activity gives an even clearer look at why strategic planning must be done at the upper levels of management. The key word here is "done." It cannot be neglected or dropped out. It cannot be *assumed* to be done. Strategic planning must be done and stated and made known at least to the next lower levels of management so coordination and correct targeting can take place.

Purpose and Strategic Planning

A strategic plan begins with the observation of a situation to be handled or a goal to be met.

It always carries with it a statement of the definite purpose or purposes to be achieved.

Once the purpose has been established, it is possible to derive from it various strategic plannings.

In fact, STRATEGY CAN BE SAID TO BE HOW ONE IS GOING TO ACTUALLY EFFECTIVELY AND SWIFTLY GET A PURPOSE MANIFESTED AND ROLLING IN THE REAL PHYSICAL UNIVERSE AT SPEED AND WITH NO FLUBS.

Any strategic plan can encompass a number of major actions required from one or more different sectors in order to achieve the purpose. These are expressed in highly general terms as they are a statement of the initial overall planning that has been done. From them one can then derive tactical plannings. But all of these things have to fit together.

Example:

Situation: The ABC Paper Company, though continuing to produce its formerly successful line of paper products, is also continuing to concentrate solely on its regular, already-established clientele while neglecting a number of its potential publics. The company is rapidly going broke and losing its execs to companies where there is "more opportunity for expansion."

Purpose: Put a full-blown paper company there which reaches all of its potential public for volume sales of existing and new products, while it also continues to sell and service its regular clientele in volume, and thus restore the company's solvency and build its repute as a lucrative, progressive concern with opportunities for expansion.

Strategic Plan: The strategic planning, based on the situation and established purpose, might go something like this:

1. The most immediate and vital action needed to arrest the losses is to (without interrupting any ongoing business or taking down or destroying any other unit) set up and get functioning a new sales unit (alongside the existing one) which will have as its first priority the development of immediate new clients for the current line of products from among (a) retail paper outlets, (b) wholesale paper outlets, and (c) direct mail order. Clean, experienced salesmen will need to be procured to head up each of these sections, and other professional salesmen will need to be located in volume. These can be hired at very low retainer and make the bulk of their money on commissions. This operation can then be expanded over broader areas using district managers, salesmen who start other salesmen and even door-to-door salesmen. As a part of this plan, commission systems, package sales kits and promotion and

advertising will need to be worked out. Getting this going on an immediate basis will boost sales and offset losses and very shortly expand the company into the field of stellar profits.

2. While the immediate holding action is going in, current sales and servicing of clients must be maintained. At the same time, sales and production records of existing staff will need to be reviewed as well as a thorough accounting done of company books to find where the losses are coming from. Any unproductive personnel will need to be dismissed and those who do produce retained. Should any embezzlement or financial irregularity be found this will need to be handled with appropriate legal action. In other words, the current operation is to be fully reviewed, cleaned up and its production not only maintained but stepped up all possible, with production targets set and met.

3. A program is to be worked out whereby surveys are done of all publics to find out what new paper products the publics want or will buy. Based on these survey results, a whole new line of paper products (additional to the old established line) can then be developed, produced, promoted and sold broadly. The program for establishing the new line of goods will need to cover financing, the organizing of the new production unit (including clean executives, competent designers, any needed additional workmen) as well as any additional machinery or equipment required. It will also need to cover broad PR, promotion and sales campaigns that push the new products as well as the old for volume sales of both. Inherent in this planning would be a campaign to enhance the company's image as pioneers in the field of new paper products with opportunities for expansion-minded executives.

Such a strategic plan not only corrects a bad situation but turns it around into a highly profitable and expanding scene for the future of the whole company.

What one is trying to accomplish is digging the scene out of the soup and expanding it into a terrific level of viability.

From this strategic plan, tactical planning would be done, taking the broad strategic targets and breaking them down into precise and exactly targeted actions which get the strategic planning executed.

One would have many people working on this and it would be essential that they all had the purpose straight and that there be no conflicting internal spots in the overall campaign. Somebody reading over such plans might not see the importance of it unless they understood the situation and had a general overall riding purpose from which they could refine their tactical planning.

It is quite common in tactical execution of a strategic planning to find it necessary to modify some tactical targets or add new ones or even drop out some as found to be unnecessary.

The tactical management of a strategic planning is a bit of an art in itself so this is allowed for.

Given a good purpose, then, against which things can be coordinated, the strategic action necessary to accomplish it can then be worked out and the tactical plans to bring the strategic plans into existence can follow.

This way a group can flourish and prosper. When all strengths and forces are aligned to a single thrust a tremendous amount of power can be developed.

So one gets the purpose stated and from that works out what strategy will be used to accomplish the purpose and this then bridges the purpose into a tactical feasibility.

When the strategic plan, with its purpose, has been put forward, it is picked up by the next lower level of command and turned into tactical planning.

Strategic Versus Tactical Planning

Strategy differs from tactics.

This is a point which must be clearly understood by the various echelons of management.

There is a very, very great difference between a strategic plan and a tactical plan.

While tactical planning is used to win an engagement, strategic planning is used to win the full campaign.

While the strategic plan is the large-scale, long-range plan to ensure victory, a tactical plan tells exactly who to move what to where and exactly what to do at that point.

The tactical plan must integrate into the strategic plan and accomplish the strategic plan. And it must do this with precise, doable targets.

And that, in essence, is management.

Bridging Between Purpose and Tactical

One error that is commonly made by untrained personnel is to jump from purpose to tactical planning, omitting the strategic plan. And this won't work. The reason it won't work is that unless one's targeted tactical plan is aligned to a strategic plan it will go off the rails.

The point to be understood here is that strategic planning *creates* tactical planning. One won't get one's purpose achieved unless there is a strategy worked out and used by which to achieve it. And, based on that strategy, one works out the tactical moves to be made to implement the strategy. But jumping from purpose to tactical, ignoring the strategy, one will miss.

So, between purpose and tactical there is *always* the step of strategic planning. We could say that by a strategic plan is meant some means to get the purpose itself to function.

It is actually a plan that has to do with cleverness.

One might be well aware of the purpose and might come up with a number of tactical targets having to do with it. And possibly the targets will work, in themselves. But the purpose is to get a situation handled and, lacking a strategic means to do this, one might still find himself facing the same problem.

Putting the actual bridge there between purpose and tactical, which bridge is the strategic side of it, the purpose will have some chance of succeeding.

BATTLE PLANS

One accomplishes his goals by formulating plans and programs, which are then done target by target. An individual or group has daily and weekly actions he must do that will result in completed targets and programs. A tool one can employ to get his programs done, plans completed and goals accomplished is *battle plans*.

A "battle plan" is defined as:

A list of targets for the coming day or week which forward the strategic planning and handle the immediate actions and outnesses which impede it. (An outness is a condition or instance of something being wrong, incorrect or missing.)

Some people write "battle plans" as just a series of actions which they hope to get done in the coming day or week. This is fine and better than nothing and does give some orientation to one's actions. In fact, someone who does not do this is quite likely to get far less done and be considerably more harassed and "busy" than one who does. An orderly planning of what one intends to do in the coming day or week and then getting it done is an excellent way to achieve production. But this is using "battle planning" in an irreducible-minimum form as a tool.

Let us take up definitions. Why is this called a "battle plan" in the first place? It seems a very harsh military term to apply to the workaday world of administration. But it is a very apt term.

A war is something that happens over a long period of time. The fate of everything depends on it. A battle is something which occurs in a short unit of time. One can lose several battles and still win a war. Thus one in essence is talking about short periods of time when one is talking about a battle plan.

This goes further. When one is talking about a war, one is talking about a series of events which will take place over a long period of time. No general, or captain for that matter, ever won a war unless he did some strategic planning. This would concern an overall conduct of a war or a sector of it.

This is the big, upper-level idea sector. It is posed in high generalities, has definite purposes and applies at the top of the Admin Scale.

Below strategic planning one has tactical. In order to carry out a strategic plan one must have the plan of movement and actions necessary to carry it out. Tactical planning normally occurs down the org board in an army and is normally used to implement strategic planning. (An *org board*, short for *organizing board*, is a board which displays the functions, duties, sequences of action and authorities of an organization.) Tactical planning can go down to a point as low as "Private Joe is to keep his machine gun pointed on clump of trees 10 and fire if anything moves in it."

"Middle management"—the heads of regiments right on down to the corporals are covered by this term—is concerned with the implementation of strategic planning.

The upper planning body turns out a strategic plan. Middle management turns this strategic plan into tactical orders. They do this on a long-term basis and a short-term basis. When you get on down to the short-term basis you have battle plans.

A battle plan therefore means turning strategic planning into exact doable targets which are then executed in terms of motion and action for the immediate period being worked on. Thus one gets a situation whereby a good strategic plan, turned into good tactical targets and then executed, results in forward progress. Enough of these sequences carried out successfully gives one the war.

This should give you a grip on what a battle plan really is. It is the list of targets to be executed in the immediate short-term future that will implement and bring into reality some portion of the strategic plan.

One can see then that management is at its best when there is a strategic plan and when it is known at least down to the level of tactical planners. And tactical planners are simply those people putting strategic plans into targets which are then known to and executed from middle management on down. This is very successful management when it is done.

Of course the worthwhileness of any evolution depends on the soundness of the strategic plan.

But the strategic plan is dependent upon programs being written in target form and which are doable within the resources available.

What we speak of as "compliance" is really a done target. The person doing the target might not be aware of the overall strategic plan or how it fits into it; however, it is very poor management indeed whose targets do not *all* implement to one degree or another the overall strategic plan.

When we speak of coordination, we are really talking about conceiving or overseeing a strategic plan into the tactical version and at the lower echelon (level of responsibility in an organization) coordinating the actions of those who will do the actual things necessary to carry it out so that they all align in one direction.

All this comes under the heading of *alignment*. As an example, if you put a number of people in a large hall facing in various directions and then suddenly yelled at them to start running, they would, of course, collide with one another and you would have a complete confusion. This is the picture one gets when strategic planning is not turned into smooth tactical planning and is not executed within that framework. These people running in this hall could get very busy, even frantic, and one could say that they were on the job and producing but that would certainly be a very large lie. Their actions are not coordinated. Now if we were to take these same people in the same hall and have them do something useful such as clean up the hall, we are dealing with specific actions of specific individuals having to do with brooms and mops—who gets them, who empties the trash and so forth. The strategic plan of "Get the hall ready for the convention" is turned into a tactical plan which says exactly who does what and where. That would be the tactical plan. The result would be a clean hall ready for the convention.

But "Clean up the hall for the convention" by simple inspection can be seen to be what would be only a small portion of an overall strategic plan. In other words the strategic plan itself has to be broken down into smaller sectors.

One can see then that a battle plan could exist for the head of an organization which would have a number of elements in it which in their turn were turned over to subexecutives who would write battle plans for their own sectors which would be far more specific. Thus we have a gradient scale of the grand overall plan broken down into segments and these segments broken down even further.

The test of all of this is whether or not it results in worthwhile accomplishments which forward the general overall strategic plan.

If you understand all the above, you will have mastered the elements of coordination.

Feasibility enters into such planning. This depends upon the resources available. Thus a certain number of targets and battle plans, to an organization which is expanding or attempting big projects, must include organizational planning and targets and battle plans so that the organization stays together as it expands. One writes a battle plan, not on the basis of, "What am I going to do tomorrow?" or, "What am I going to do next week?" (which is fine in its own way and better than nothing), but on the overall question, "What exact actions do I have to do to carry out this strategic plan to achieve the exact results necessary for this stage of the strategic plan within the limits of available resources?" Then one would have the battle plan for the next day or the next week.

There is one thing to beware of in doing battle plans. One can write a great many targets which have little or nothing to do with the strategic plan and which keep people terribly busy and which accomplish no part of the overall strategic plan. Thus a battle plan can become a liability since it is not pushing any overall strategic plan and is not accomplishing any tactical objective.

So what is a "battle plan"? It is the doable targets in written form which accomplish a desirable part of an overall strategic plan.

The understanding and competent use of targeting in battle plans is vital to the overall accomplishment that raises production, income, delivery or anything else that is a desirable end.

It is a test of an executive whether or not he can competently battle plan and then get his battle plan executed. This tool can also be applied by persons in all walks of life and in any activity.

One accomplishes goals by formulating plans. To implement the plans one does programs and projects, which get completed through the use of battle plans. This aligns to the Admin Scale.

GOALS

The largest, most successful construction company in the state.

PURPOSES

To furnish affordable, good quality housing in this part of the country.

POLICY

Stress quality of workmanship at all times.

Adhere to building codes of the area in which we are building.

STRATEGIC PLAN

To expand the construction company in other parts of the state by building new housing developments in the fastest-growing cities in each area.

PROGRAM

New Housing Development Program

PROJECT

Build Foundations Project

PROJECT

Frame Houses Project

IDEAL SCENE

Houses being constructed on time and within budget.

ORDERS

Dig the trench for the south wall of the foundation for lot #27.

MONDAY BATTLE PLAN

1. Lay out foundations for lots 27–31.

2. Excavate foundations for lots 27–31.

3. Schedule the concrete pour for lots 27–31 for Tuesday.

4. Report target #5 of project complete.

STATISTICS

of Houses Built

ORDERS

Nail the wood supports with 3½" nails.

MONDAY BATTLE PLAN

1. Cut all lumber to length for units 18–22.

2. Lay out the walls for units 18–22.

3. Assemble the four main walls for units 18–22.

4. Erect and brace the four main walls for units 18–22.

5. Report target #11 of project as done.

VALUABLE FINAL PRODUCT

Maxims of Programing

Programing is important enough to pay a lot of attention to. And there is a lot of information about it. And the facts all add up to no matter how many programs you have, each one consists of certain parts. And if you don't assemble those parts and run the program in an orderly fashion, then it just won't spark off. These are some of the principles about programs.

If you don't know these facts of life, here they are:

Maxim One: Any idea, no matter if badly executed, is better than no idea at all.

Maxim Two: A program, to be effective, must be executed.

Maxim Three: A program put into action requires guidance.

Maxim Four: A program running without guidance will fail and is better left undone. If you haven't got the time to guide it, don't do it; put more steam behind existing programs because it will flop.

Maxim Five: Any program requires some finance. Get the finance into sight before you start to fire, or have a very solid guarantee that the program will produce finance before you execute it.

Maxim Six: A program requires attention from somebody. An untended program that is everybody's child will become a juvenile delinquent.

Maxim Seven: The best program is the one that will reach the greatest number of dynamics and will do the greatest good on the greatest number of dynamics. (A dynamic is an urge to survive along a certain course. There are eight dynamics: first, self; second, sex and the family unit; third, groups; fourth, mankind; fifth, life forms; sixth, physical universe; seventh, spirits; and eighth, Supreme Being. These dynamics embrace all the goals of survival an individual has and all the things for which he survives.)

Maxim Eight: Programs must support themselves financially.

Maxim Nine: Programs must *accumulate* interest and bring in other assistance by the virtue of the program interest alone or they will never grow.

Maxim Ten: A program is a bad program if it detracts from programs which are already proving successful or distracts staff people or associates from work they are already doing that is adding up to successful execution of other programs.

Maxim Eleven: Never spend more on a program than the income from one person can repay.

Maxim Twelve: Never permit a new program to inhibit the success of a routine one or injure its income.

Programing requires execution. It requires carry-through. It requires judgment enough to know a good program and carry it on and on and to recognize a bad one and drop it like hot bricks.

Programs extend in time and go overdue to the extent the various types of targets are not set or not pushed home or drop out. They fail only because the various types of targets are not executed or are not kept in.

You can get done almost anything you want to do if types of targets are understood, set with reality, held in or completed.

One can readily accomplish the intended goals either for himself or for his group by adherence to good, steady programing that wins.

This is the way to make planning an actuality, to achieve goals. It is as true for an individual as it is for a large group. All people can benefit from this technology.■

PRACTICAL EXERCISES

Here are some practical exercises to increase your knowledge and skill in applying the basic data on programs and targets to achieve your goals.

1 Work out and write down a realistic goal you want to achieve in some area of your life, job, etc.

2 Write up an example of strategic planning you would do to accomplish the goal you set in the previous practical exercise.

3 Write down two examples of each of the following target types. Each example is to be one that could be on a program you would write and do.

> a. major target
>
> b. primary target
>
> c. vital target
>
> d. operating target
>
> e. conditional target
>
> f. production target

4 Do the program given as Sample Program #1 in this booklet. Actually carry out its steps as directed in the program.

5 Do the program given as Sample Program #2 in this booklet. Actually carry out its steps as directed in the program.

6 Write a program to take a walk. Use the target types you learned in this booklet to do so.

7 Write a program to get ready for the day. Lay out the steps you take to prepare for your day of work, study or whatever. Use the target types you learned in this booklet to do so.

8 Write a program that would be done to accomplish the strategic planning you set down in doing Practical Exercise #2 above. Utilize the materials you read in this booklet and the skills you gained in doing the above practical exercises.

9 Write up a battle plan for the day which will forward the strategic planning and program you have written in exercises 2 and 8 above.

RESULTS FROM APPLICATION

Failure to accomplish one's goals—personal, familial or organizational—has been a heavy burden many people have had to bear. L. Ron Hubbard's discoveries on the subject of target attainment, however, can provide any individual with methods to lift this weight and thus create a more fulfilling life. In fact, those who have studied and applied these tenets have attained success, where such seemed difficult or impossible to reach before. Below you will find just a few tributes to the workability of Mr. Hubbard's developments in this field.

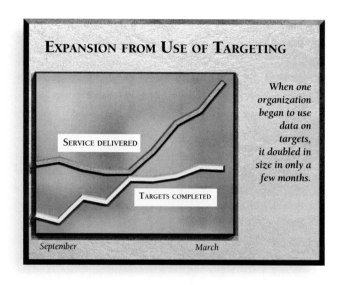

EXPANSION FROM USE OF TARGETING

SERVICE DELIVERED

TARGETS COMPLETED

September   March

When one organization began to use data on targets, it doubled in size in only a few months.

A young woman from Italy got a job that consisted of carrying out long-term projects. She said about it:

"I used to not be able to confront doing big jobs that would take many weeks to get done and required a lot of steps to get the overall job done. Then I found out about target types and how to use them. Now, when I have a big project in front of me, I sit down and I break it down into targets and as I get each of them done I know I am getting closer and closer to achieving the complete product. Every target done is a win."

Employed as Communications Officer in a large US corporation, a man was made responsible for the international communication lines. When first starting the job, he found a situation where many units in his charge had antiquated communication systems or even none at all. This is how he went about handling it:

"My knowledge of this area was almost nonexistent and the financial budget was limited. This involved, altogether, fifty units that had to be handled.

"From this I worked out the exact plan for the fifty units and how to get all these units equipped with proper, fast-running communications systems. I then wrote programs using Mr. Hubbard's technology on targets and with this series of programs, I was able to procure, install and make these systems functional. In addition I wrote a program for the nine main areas to give them directions for better operation in their respective areas.

"Pushing the targets through to completion, with dogged persistence, I accomplished what had not been done before and every unit ended up with a computerized fast-running communications system. The best ever. It would have been almost impossible to get this

done in the time it was done without the use of targeting technology."

One lady, whose family and many of her friends were in another state, was still able to continue her relationships and help them by use of targets and goals:

"I set goals last year to accomplish certain things with my family. I decided what I wanted to do to help my parents and my friends. I set the major targets that we wanted to accomplish, then we set the other different types of targets and I went over this with them. We agreed we would do these things, small things or large, to help us get closer together.

"Now my son can read and is very proud of this. My husband has completed things in his life he has long planned to do and is doing much better as a result. My family is moving closer to where I live and we have had time together and helped each other despite the distance in the meanwhile. My friends are each doing better and I have helped them through support and other small things to really push those targets through that they had set for themselves. These small things add to and make my life full and keep me in balance.

"Sure, I target for production on the job and for business projects. But being able to help someone else to complete targets in their lives gives me a great feeling of knowing I helped. Knowing this technology, I can get things done on a long-distance line and accomplish targets that bring my family closer together."

An executive for personnel in the Los Angeles area had a major task to perform in order to build up a second unit for a film studio. Here is how she handled this:

"I was given a specific deadline to hire a large number of staff and professionals in a very short time period.

"At first, I didn't really know how to go about getting this done within the time frame I had, or if I could get it done at all. I knew it was important to complete it within the amount of time I had. In fact, four people prior to me had attempted to achieve the same deadline that I had just been given.

"I worked with other employees; I tried to get them to achieve this over and over but I wasn't getting anywhere. Finally, I realized that there must be some technology that I wasn't applying.

"I looked to L. Ron Hubbard's targeting technology.

"I then really figured out what exactly I had to do to get the product. I named who I wanted to hire and I wrote a program with the exact targets that I had to do in order to get all of these people actually arrived to work. I then met with every person, giving each one an exact project to execute so all of them would arrive within the required time.

"This worked. The whole team knew exactly what part of the product they were responsible for, how much time they had to get their part of the product produced and I got each step to hire each person done one by one and this made it possible for us to attain our goal!

"We achieved our major target! We got the whole program done within the needed amount of time. I couldn't have done this without knowing and applying this technology."

An executive in a Southern California construction project found Mr. Hubbard's technology on programs and targets of immense value in accomplishing his intended goals:

"We had to get new buildings constructed as they were badly needed to dramatically improve the facilities of our organization. Our construction plans required approval by a specific time to ensure our success. L. Ron Hubbard's discoveries on target types and programs were used to isolate the exact actions that had to be accomplished and in what sequence. What I personally found of tremendous help was that Mr. Hubbard discovered and differentiated the different types of targets. This technology allows one to go from wherever he is to where he wants to go by properly using each type of target.

"We had to obtain agreement for the construction plan from the local community. Our program had targets to find out what the community leaders wanted so we could provide this and obtain the authorizations we needed. Had we not done this, we would not have been able to build what we wanted. But because we were applying Mr. Hubbard's technology on programs and targets, we easily handled what was required and obtained full approval. As a result, everyone won.

"Anyone trying to get anything done in this world is going to run aground unless he knows and uses Mr. Hubbard's technology on target types and programs. It is based on natural laws. It is how one gets something accomplished. It will help spot and handle the potential pitfalls before one is stopped by them. It points out the things that, if not maintained throughout executing the construction plan, would snarl up the whole plan.

"Anything can be done using this tech. Literally anything!"

Just using the rudiments of Mr. Hubbard's technology on the Admin Scale and programing can have astounding results.

"Using the Admin Scale, I quickly isolated the primary goal I was reaching for in life. Then, using what I'd learned in just one article by L. Ron Hubbard on programing, I laid out how I was going to achieve my goal. I found my life catapulting forward in the direction I wanted it to go.

"My business began expanding at a rapid rate and became the largest of its type in the world. Even the time frame that I had roughly sketched out in my plan came off almost to the day. When I started, I hadn't any idea how to get where I wanted to go and had no confidence that I ever would or could. But learning these basics opened the door and literally changed the course of my life."

Using the Admin Scale developed by L. Ron Hubbard to lay a good foundation for marriage proved to be very worthwhile for this couple:

"My wife and I have been very happily married now for more than twelve years. Prior to getting married, we sat down and did Admin Scales together and ensured that these were well aligned. The result has been a very stable and rewarding marriage without arguments or fights or any of the many common marital troubles."

A graphic artist working in a busy design studio was able to get a large volume of work done without being dispersed by the many different demands and projects at hand.

"Without a daily battle plan at work (and even for my days off!) I would be lost and dispersed. Writing a correct, accurate and doable battle plan for each week and day, I am able to accomplish all the things that I want and need to get done. It's really amazing what order this one basic Scientology datum has put into my life."

Carrying a dream through to reality became possible for an Australian woman using Mr. Hubbard's Administrative Technology.

"I did an Admin Scale for my personal life and laid out every step of it, including a program to create a successful marriage.

"After about three or four weeks nothing was happening and I thought to myself (foolishly) 'This doesn't work.' Then I realized that I was not **doing** my program! I started executing the targets I had set. It took some confront on my part but I approached my first 'prospect' and bravely stated that I wanted to get to know him. I had already imagined how he would say, 'Well, I like you a lot, but strictly as a friend.' Of course I had worked out my ready reply: 'Okay, that's fine. I was just checking it out.'

"Well, to my surprise, he said, 'Hey, that sounds like a good idea. Let's get to know each other.'

"I was in shock!

"I carried through with the rest of the targets on the program I'd drawn up. The end result is that I'm married to a great guy who is everything I wanted; we have been happily married for nine years.

"When I recently looked over that first Admin Scale (I kept it, of course!) I saw that I've achieved all the points I had set down and more.

"This is a great piece of technology that works like a dream."

GLOSSARY

Admin Scale: short for *Administrative Scale,* a scale which gives a sequence (and relative seniority) of subjects relating to organization: goals, purposes, policy, plans, programs, projects, orders, ideal scenes, statistics, valuable final products. Each of these must operate in a coordinated manner to achieve success in the intended accomplishment of an envisioned goal. This scale is used to help one align them.

affinity: love, liking or any other emotional attitude; the degree of liking. The basic definition of affinity is the consideration of distance, whether good or bad.

battle plan: a series of exact doable targets for the coming day or week which forward the strategic planning of an individual or a group.

communication: an interchange of ideas across space between two individuals.

communication line: the route along which a communication travels from one person to another.

confront: to face without flinching or avoiding. The ability to confront is actually the ability to be there comfortably and perceive.

dynamic: an urge to survive along a certain course; an urge toward existence in an area of life. There are eight dynamics: first, self; second, sex and the family unit; third, groups; fourth, mankind; fifth, life forms; sixth, physical universe; seventh, spirits; and eighth, Supreme Being.

gradient: a gradual approach to something taken step by step, level by level, each step or level being, of itself, easily attainable— so that finally, complicated and difficult activities can be achieved with relative ease. The term *gradient* also applies to each of the steps taken in such an approach.

org board: short for *organizing board,* a board which displays the functions, duties, communication routes, sequences of action and authorities of an organization. It shows the pattern of organizing to obtain a product.

outness: a condition or instance of something being wrong, incorrect or missing.

Scientology: an applied religious philosophy developed by L. Ron Hubbard. It is the study and handling of the spirit in relationship to itself, universes and other life. The word *Scientology* comes from the Latin *scio,* which means "know" and the Greek word *logos,* meaning "the word or outward form by which the inward thought is expressed and made known." Thus, Scientology means knowing about knowing.

terminal: a person, point or position which can receive, relay or send a communication.

ABOUT
L. RON HUBBARD

No more fitting statement typifies the life of L. Ron Hubbard than his simple declaration: "I like to help others and count it as my greatest pleasure in life to see a person free himself from the shadows which darken his days." Behind these pivotal words stands a lifetime of service to mankind and a legacy of wisdom that enables anyone to attain long-cherished dreams of happiness and spiritual freedom.

Born in Tilden, Nebraska on March 13, 1911, his road of discovery and dedication to his fellows began at an early age. "I wanted other people to be happy, and could not understand why they weren't," he wrote of his youth; and therein lay the sentiments that would long guide his steps. By the age of nineteen, he had traveled more than a quarter of a million miles, examining the cultures of Java, Japan, India and the Philippines.

Returning to the United States in 1929, Ron resumed his formal education and studied mathematics, engineering and the then new field of nuclear physics—all providing vital tools for continued research. To finance that research, Ron embarked upon a literary career in the early 1930s, and soon became one of the most widely read authors of popular fiction. Yet never losing sight of his primary goal, he continued his mainline research through extensive travel and expeditions.

With the advent of World War II, he entered the United States Navy as a lieutenant (junior grade) and served as commander of antisubmarine corvettes. Left partially blind and lame from injuries sustained during combat, he was diagnosed as permanently disabled by 1945. Through application of his theories on the mind, however, he was not only able to help fellow servicemen, but also to regain his own health.

After five more years of intensive research, Ron's discoveries were presented to the world in *Dianetics: The Modern Science of Mental Health*. The first popular handbook on the human mind expressly written for the man in the street, *Dianetics* ushered in a new era of hope for mankind and a new

phase of life for its author. He did, however, not cease his research, and as breakthrough after breakthrough was carefully codified through late 1951, the applied religious philosophy of Scientology was born.

Because Scientology explains the whole of life, there is no aspect of man's existence that L. Ron Hubbard's subsequent work did not address. Residing variously in the United States and England, his continued research brought forth solutions to such social ills as declining educational standards and pandemic drug abuse.

All told, L. Ron Hubbard's works on Scientology and Dianetics total forty million words of recorded lectures, books and writings. Together, these constitute the legacy of a lifetime that ended on January 24, 1986. Yet the passing of L. Ron Hubbard in no way constituted an end; for with a hundred million of his books in circulation and millions of people daily applying his technologies for betterment, it can truly be said the world still has no greater friend. ■

CHURCHES OF SCIENTOLOGY
Contact Your Nearest Church or Organization or visit www.volunteerministers.org

UNITED STATES

ALBUQUERQUE
Church of Scientology
8106 Menaul Boulevard NE
Albuquerque, New Mexico
87110

ANN ARBOR
Church of Scientology
66 E. Michigan Avenue
Battle Creek, Michigan 49017

ATLANTA
Church of Scientology
1611 Mt. Vernon Road
Dunwoody, Georgia 30338

AUSTIN
Church of Scientology
2200 Guadalupe
Austin, Texas 78705

BOSTON
Church of Scientology
448 Beacon Street
Boston, Massachusetts 02115

BUFFALO
Church of Scientology
836 Main Street
Buffalo, New York 14202

CHICAGO
Church of Scientology
3011 North Lincoln Avenue
Chicago, Illinois 60657-4207

CINCINNATI
Church of Scientology
215 West 4th Street, 5th Floor
Cincinnati, Ohio 45202-2670

CLEARWATER
Church of Scientology
Flag Service Organization
210 South Fort Harrison Avenue
Clearwater, Florida 33756

Foundation Church of
Scientology
Flag Ship Service Organization
c/o *Freewinds* Relay Office
118 North Fort Harrison Avenue
Clearwater, Florida 33755-4013

COLUMBUS
Church of Scientology
30 North High Street
Columbus, Ohio 43215

DALLAS
Church of Scientology
Celebrity Centre Dallas
1850 North Buckner Boulevard
Dallas, Texas 75228

DENVER
Church of Scientology
3385 South Bannock Street
Englewood, Colorado 80110

DETROIT
Church of Scientology
28000 Middlebelt Road
Farmington Hills, Michigan
48334

HONOLULU
Church of Scientology
1146 Bethel Street
Honolulu, Hawaii 96813

KANSAS CITY
Church of Scientology
3619 Broadway
Kansas City, Missouri 64111

LAS VEGAS
Church of Scientology
846 East Sahara Avenue
Las Vegas, Nevada 89104

Church of Scientology
Celebrity Centre Las Vegas
4850 W. Flamingo Road, Suite 10
Las Vegas, Nevada 89103

LONG ISLAND
Church of Scientology
64 Bethpage Road
Hicksville, New York
11801-2850

LOS ANGELES AND VICINITY
Church of Scientology
of Los Angeles
4810 Sunset Boulevard
Los Angeles, California 90027

Church of Scientology
1451 Irvine Boulevard
Tustin, California 92680

Church of Scientology
1277 East Colorado Boulevard
Pasadena, California 91106

Church of Scientology
15643 Sherman Way
Van Nuys, California 91406

Church of Scientology
American Saint Hill
Organization
1413 L. Ron Hubbard Way
Los Angeles, California 90027

Church of Scientology
American Saint Hill Foundation
1413 L. Ron Hubbard Way
Los Angeles, California 90027

Church of Scientology
Advanced Organization
of Los Angeles
1306 L. Ron Hubbard Way
Los Angeles, California 90027

Church of Scientology
Celebrity Centre International
5930 Franklin Avenue
Hollywood, California 90028

LOS GATOS
Church of Scientology
650 Saratoga Avenue
San Jose, California 95117

MIAMI
Church of Scientology
120 Giralda Avenue
Coral Gables, Florida 33134

MINNEAPOLIS
Church of Scientology
Twin Cities
1011 Nicollet Mall
Minneapolis, Minnesota 55403

MOUNTAIN VIEW
Church of Scientology
2483 Old Middlefield Way
Mountain View, California
94043

NASHVILLE
Church of Scientology
Celebrity Centre Nashville
1204 16th Avenue South
Nashville, Tennessee 37212

NEW HAVEN
Church of Scientology
909 Whalley Avenue
New Haven, Connecticut
06515-1728

NEW YORK CITY
Church of Scientology
227 West 46th Street
New York, New York
10036-1409

Church of Scientology
Celebrity Centre New York
65 East 82nd Street
New York, New York 10028

ORLANDO
Church of Scientology
1830 East Colonial Drive
Orlando, Florida 32803-4729

PHILADELPHIA
Church of Scientology
1315 Race Street
Philadelphia, Pennsylvania
19107

PHOENIX
Church of Scientology
2702 N. 44th st. Suite A100
Phoenix, Arizona 85038

PORTLAND
Church of Scientology
2636 NE Sandy Boulevard
Portland, Oregon 97232-2342

Church of Scientology
Celebrity Centre Portland
708 SW Salmon Street
Portland, Oregon 97205

SACRAMENTO
Church of Scientology
825 15th Street
Sacramento, California
95814-2096

SALT LAKE CITY
Church of Scientology
1931 South 1100 East
Salt Lake City, Utah 84106

SAN DIEGO
Church of Scientology
1330 4th Avenue
San Diego, California 92101

SAN FRANCISCO
Church of Scientology
701 Montomery Street
San Francisco, California 94111

SAN JOSE
Church of Scientology
80 East Rosemary Street
San Jose, California 95112

SANTA BARBARA
Church of Scientology
524 State Street
Santa Barbara, California 93101

SEATTLE
Church of Scientology
2226 3rd Avenue
Seattle, Washington 98121

ST. LOUIS
Church of Scientology
6901 Delmar Boulevard
University City, Missouri 63130

TAMPA
Church of Scientology
3102 N. Havana Avenue
Tampa, Florida 33607

WASHINGTON, DC
Founding Church of Scientology
of Washington, DC
1701 20th Street NW
Washington, DC 20009

PUERTO RICO

HATO REY
Dianetics Center of Puerto Rico
272 JT Piñero Avenue
Hyde Park
San Juan, Puerto Rico 00918

CANADA

EDMONTON
Church of Scientology
10206 106th Street NW
Edmonton, Alberta
Canada T5J 1H7

KITCHENER
Church of Scientology
104 King Street West, 2nd Floor
Kitchener, Ontario
Canada N2G 1A6

MONTREAL
Church of Scientology
4489 Papineau Street
Montreal, Quebec
Canada H2H 1T7

OTTAWA
Church of Scientology
150 Rideau Street, 2nd Floor
Ottawa, Ontario
Canada K1N 5X6

QUEBEC
Church of Scientology
350 Bd Chareste Est
Quebec, Quebec
Canada G1K 3H5

TORONTO
Church of Scientology
696 Yonge Street, 2nd Floor
Toronto, Ontario
Canada M4Y 2A7

VANCOUVER
Church of Scientology
401 West Hastings Street
Vancouver, British Columbia
Canada V6B 1L5

WINNIPEG
Church of Scientology
315 Garry Street, Suite 210
Winnipeg, Manitoba
Canada R3B 2G7

UNITED KINGDOM

BIRMINGHAM
Church of Scientology
8 Ethel Street
Winston Churchill House
Birmingham, England B2 4BG

BRIGHTON
Church of Scientology
Third Floor, 79-83 North Street
Brighton, Sussex
England BN1 1ZA

EAST GRINSTEAD
Church of Scientology
Saint Hill Foundation
Saint Hill Manor
East Grinstead, West Sussex
England RH19 4JY

Advanced Organization
Saint Hill
Saint Hill Manor
East Grinstead, West Sussex
England RH19 4JY

EDINBURGH
Hubbard Academy of Personal
Independence
20 Southbridge
Edinburgh, Scotland EH1 1LL

LONDON
Church of Scientology
68 Tottenham Court Road
London, England W1P 0BB

Church of Scientology
Celebrity Centre London
42 Leinster Gardens
London, England W2 3AN

MANCHESTER
Church of Scientology
258 Deansgate
Manchester, England M3 4BG

PLYMOUTH
Church of Scientology
41 Ebrington Street
Plymouth, Devon
England PL4 9AA

SUNDERLAND
Church of Scientology
51 Fawcett Street
Sunderland, Tyne and Wear
England SR1 1RS

AUSTRALIA

ADELAIDE
Church of Scientology
24–28 Waymouth Street
Adelaide, South Australia
Australia 5000

BRISBANE
Church of Scientology
106 Edward Street, 2nd Floor
Brisbane, Queensland
Australia 4000

CANBERRA
Church of Scientology
43–45 East Row
Canberra City, ACT
Australia 2601

MELBOURNE
Church of Scientology
42–44 Russell Street
Melbourne, Victoria
Australia 3000

PERTH
Church of Scientology
108 Murray Street, 1st Floor
Perth, Western Australia
Australia 6000

SYDNEY
Church of Scientology
201 Castlereagh Street
Sydney, New South Wales
Australia 2000

Church of Scientology
Advanced Organization
Saint Hill Australia,
New Zealand and Oceania
19–37 Greek Street
Glebe, New South Wales
Australia 2037

NEW ZEALAND

AUCKLAND
Church of Scientology
159 Queen Street, 3rd Floor
Auckland 1, New Zealand

AFRICA

BULAWAYO
Church of Scientology
Southampton House, Suite 202
Main Street and 9th Avenue
Bulawayo, Zimbabwe

CAPE TOWN
Church of Scientology
Ground Floor, Dorlane House
39 Roeland Street
Cape Town 8001, South Africa

DURBAN
Church of Scientology
20 Buckingham Terrace
Westville, Durban 3630
South Africa

HARARE
Church of Scientology
404-409 Pockets Building
50 Jason Moyo Avenue
Harare, Zimbabwe

JOHANNESBURG
Church of Scientology
4th Floor, Budget House
130 Main Street
Johannesburg 2001
South Africa

Church of Scientology
No. 108 1st Floor,
Bordeaux Centre
Gordon Road, Corner Jan
Smuts Avenue
Blairgowrie, Randburg 2125
South Africa

PORT ELIZABETH
Church of Scientology
2 St. Christopher's
27 Westbourne Road Central
Port Elizabeth 6001
South Africa

PRETORIA
Church of Scientology
307 Ancore Building
Corner Jeppe and Esselen Streets
Sunnyside, Pretoria 0002
South Africa

SCIENTOLOGY MISSIONS

INTERNATIONAL OFFICE
Scientology Missions
International
6331 Hollywood Boulevard
Suite 501
Los Angeles, California
90028-6314

UNITED STATES
Scientology Missions
International
Western United States Office
1308 L. Ron Hubbard Way
Los Angeles, California 90027

Scientology Missions
International
Eastern United States Office
349 W. 48th Street
New York, New York 10036

Scientology Missions
International
Flag Land Base Office
210 South Fort Harrison Avenue
Clearwater, Florida 33756

AFRICA
Scientology Missions
International
African Office
6th Floor, Budget House
130 Main Street
Johannesburg 2001
South Africa

AUSTRALIA, NEW ZEALAND AND OCEANIA
Scientology Missions
International
Australian, New Zealand
and Oceanian Office
201 Castlereagh Street, 3rd Flr.
Sydney, New South Wales
Australia 2000

CANADA
Scientology Missions
International
Canadian Office
696 Yonge Street
Toronto, Ontario
Canada M4Y 2A7

UNITED KINGDOM
Scientology Missions
International
United Kingdom Office
Saint Hill Manor
East Grinstead, West Sussex,
England RH19 4JY

TO OBTAIN ANY BOOKS OR CAS-
SETTES BY L. RON HUBBARD WHICH
ARE NOT AVAILABLE AT YOUR LOCAL
ORGANIZATION, CONTACT ANY OF
THE FOLLOWING PUBLICATIONS
ORGANIZATIONS WORLDWIDE:

BRIDGE PUBLICATIONS, INC.
4751 Fountain Avenue
Los Angeles, California 90029
www.bridgepub.com

NEW ERA PUBLICATIONS INTERNATIONAL ApS
Store Kongensgade 53
1264 Copenhagen K
Denmark
www.newerapublications.com

BUILD A BETTER WORLD

BECOME A VOLUNTEER MINISTER

Help bring happiness, purpose and truth to your fellow man.
Become a Volunteer Minister.

Thousands of Volunteer Ministers bring relief and sanity to others all over the world using techniques like the ones found in this booklet. But more help is needed. Your help. As a Volunteer Minister you can today handle things which seemed impossible yesterday. And you can vastly improve this world's tomorrow.

Become a Volunteer Minister and brighten the world to a better place for you to live. It's easy to do. For help and information about becoming a Volunteer Minister, visit our website today. www.volunteerministers.org

You can also call or write your nearest Volunteer Ministers International organization.

VOLUNTEER MINISTERS INTERNATIONAL
A DEPARTMENT OF THE INTERNATIONAL HUBBARD ECCLESIASTICAL LEAGUE OF PASTORS

INTERNATIONAL OFFICE
6331 Hollywood Boulevard, Suite 708
Los Angeles, California 90028
Tel: (323) 960-3560 (800) 435-7498

WESTERN US
1308 L. Ron Hubbard Way
Los Angeles, California 90027
Tel: (323) 953-3357
1-888-443-5760
ihelpwestus@earthlink.net

EASTERN US
349 W. 48th Street
New York, New York 10036
Tel: (212) 757-9610
1-888-443-5788

CANADA
696 Yonge Street
Toronto, Ontario
Canada M4Y 2A7
Tel: (416) 968-0070

LATIN AMERICA
Federación Mexicana de
  Dianética, A.C.
Puebla #31
Colonia Roma, CP 06700
Mexico, D.F.
Tel: 525-511-4452

EUROPE
Store Kongensgade 55
1264 Copenhagen K
Denmark
Tel: 45-33-737-322

ITALY
Via Cadorna, 61
20090 Vimodrone (MI)
Italy
Tel: 39-0227-409-246

AUSTRALIA
201 Castlereagh Street
3rd Floor
Sydney, New South Wales
Australia 2000
Tel: 612-9267-6422

AFRICA
6th Floor, Budget House
130 Main Street
Johannesburg 2001
South Africa
Tel: 083-331-7170

UNITED KINGDOM
Saint Hill Manor
East Grinstead, West Sussex
England RH19 4JY
Tel: 44-1342-301-895

HUNGARY
1438 Budapest
PO Box 351, Hungary
Tel: 361-321-5298

COMMONWEALTH OF INDEPENDENT STATES
c/o Hubbard Humanitarian
  Center
Ul. Borisa Galushkina 19A
129301 Moscow, Russia
Tel: 7-095-961-3414

TAIWAN
2F, 65, Sec. 4
Ming-Sheng East Road
Taipei, Taiwan ROC
Tel: 88-628-770-5074

www.volunteerministers.org

Bridge Publications, Inc.
4751 Fountain Avenue, Los Angeles, California 90029
ISBN 0-88404-924-8

An L. RON HUBBARD Publication